IF FOUND PLE

C000096957

_____

⊠ _____

▯ _____

Greater Than a Tourist Book Series
Reviews from Readers

I think the series is wonderful and beneficial for tourists to get information before visiting the city. - Seckin Zumbul, Izmir Turkey

I am a world traveler who has read many trip guides but this one really made a difference for me. I would call it a heartfelt creation of a local guide expert instead of just a guide. -Susy, Isla Holbox, Mexico

New to the area like me, this is a must have! -Joe, Bloomington, USA

This is a good series that gets down to it when looking for things to do at your destination without having to read a novel for just a few ideas. -Rachel, Monterey, USA

Good information to have to plan my trip to this destination. -Pennie Farrell, Mexico

Great ideas for a port day. -Mary Martin USA

Aptly titled, you won't just be a tourist after reading this book. You'll be greater than a tourist! -Alan Warner, Grand Rapids, USA

Even though I only have three days to spend in San Miguel in an upcoming visit, I will use the author's suggestions to guide some of my time there. An easy read - with chapters named to guide me in directions I want to go. -Robert Catapano, USA

Great insights from a local perspective! Useful information and a very good value! -Sarah, USA

This series provides an in-depth experience through the eyes of a local. Reading these series will help you to travel the city in with confidence and it'll make your journey a unique one. -Andrew Teoh, Ipoh, Malaysia

GREATER THAN A TOURIST – HAMILTON ONTARIO CANADA

50 Travel Tips from a Local

Robert Ermeta

Cover designed by: Ivana Stamenkovic
Cover Image:
https://en.wikipedia.org/wiki/Hamilton,_Ontario#/media/File:HamiltonOntarioS
kylineC.JPG

Greater Than a Tourist
Visit our website at www.GreaterThanaTourist.com

Lock Haven, PA
All rights reserved.
ISBN: 9781983308918

>TOURIST

50 TRAVEL TIPS FROM A LOCAL

BOOK DESCRIPTION

Are you excited about planning your next trip?

Do you want to try something new?

Would you like some guidance from a local?

If you answered yes to any of these questions, then this Greater Than a Tourist book is for you.

Greater Than a Tourist- Hamilton, Ontario, Canada by Robert Ermeta offers the inside scoop on Hamilton. Most travel books tell you how to travel like a tourist. Although there is nothing wrong with that, as part of the Greater Than a Tourist series, this book will give you travel tips from someone who has lived at your next travel destination.

In these pages, you will discover advice that will help you throughout your stay. This book will not tell you exact addresses or store hours but instead will give you excitement and knowledge from a local that you may not find in other smaller print travel books.

Travel like a local. Slow down, stay in one place, and get to know the people and the culture. By the time you finish this book, you will be eager and prepared to travel to your next destination.

TABLE OF CONTENTS

NOTES

DEDICATION

This book is dedicated to my parents, Ron and Joni, whose perseverance and drive I inherited. Their words of encouragement, and their trust in my many educational changes, were very much needed.

To my sister, Rebecca, who always seemed to believe in me, even when I didn't. I don't always show my gratitude, but I am thankful to have you as my sister. Your graduation gift to me is what awoke a new passion, which I have now followed.

To my Husband, Cody, for supporting me through each and every endeavor I take (and there have been a lot). I may not make things easy, with my constant changes in both career paths and educational endeavors, but you have to admit I keep things interesting.

And, to my best friend, Tasha, who constantly pushed me to follow my dreams. Your friendship means the world to me, and your constant words of encouragement keep me going. Thank You.

ABOUT THE AUTHOR

We've all watched those movies where the story takes place in a small town with white picket fences, and old style housing. Some movies that come to mind are *Practical Magic, Hocus Pocus,* and *E.T.* While Hamilton, Ontario may not be considered a small town, it has always had that small town feel.

A recent Graduate from McMaster University and Mohawk College, Robert Ermeta has been a resident of Hamilton, Ontario all his life. While he always had the urge to move on to other areas of the Province and the Country, he stayed put in Hamilton; to him, Hamilton is, and always will be, home.

Robert lives on the West Hamilton Mountain with his Husband Cody, and three (yes, three) cats: Tiah, Bynx, and Milo. From his balcony you can get a clear view of the entire city. From the tree tops on the mountain, to the high rises in the downtown core, you can see it all.

Robert works as a manager for a local entertainment company, and also runs a bakery and catering business out of his home. When he has spare time he enjoys taking in the local scenery that Hamilton has to offer, sipping a coffee from the numerous shops, and hanging around down by the bay.

The old historic houses in Hamilton's downtown help feed Robert's architectural interests, and the various historical spots help to keep Hamilton's history alive.

While Hamilton may not be the first place that you think of when deciding to travel to Canada, the waterfront, hiking trails, and sound of trickling waterfalls will change your mind! After all, Hamilton is the Waterfall capital of the *World*.

HOW TO USE THIS BOOK

The Greater Than a Tourist book series was written by someone who has lived in an area for over three months. The goal of this book is to help travelers either dream or experience different locations by providing opinions from a local. The author has made suggestions based on their own experiences. Please do your own research before traveling to the area in case the suggested places are unavailable.

FROM THE PUBLISHER

Traveling can be one of the most important parts of a person's life. The anticipation and memories that you have are some of the best. As a publisher of the Greater Than a Tourist book series, as well as the popular 50 Things to Know book series, we strive to help you learn about new places, spark your imagination, and inspire you. Wherever you are and whatever you do I wish you safe, fun, and inspiring travel.

Lisa Rusczyk Ed. D.
CZYK Publishing

OUR STORY

Traveling is a passion of the "Greater than a Tourist" series creator. Lisa studied abroad in college, and for their honeymoon Lisa and her husband toured Europe. During her travels to Malta, an older man tried to give her some advice based on his own experience living on the island since he was a young boy. She was not sure if she should talk to the stranger but was interested in his advice. When traveling to some places she was wary to talk to locals because she was afraid that they weren't being genuine. Through her travels, Lisa learned how much locals had to share with tourists. Lisa created the "Greater Than a Tourist" book series to help connect people with locals. A topic that locals are very passionate about sharing.

WELCOME TO
> TOURIST

11

"Twenty years from now you will be more disappointed by the things that you didn't do than by the ones you did do. So throw off the bowlines. Sail away from the safe harbor. Catch the trade winds in your sails. Explore. Dream. Discover."

– Mark Twain

HAMILTON'S HISTORY

1. WHY VISIT HAMILTON

While Hamilton may not be your first thought when deciding to take a Canadian vacation, it is my hopes that this book will change your mind. Hamilton has a rich history, and culture, that are not very well known by those who live outside of the city and surrounding area. We had involvement in the War of 1812, we are the largest Industrial city in Ontario, and one of the largest in Canada, and we happen to be known as the waterfall capital of the world (which is no small feat).

While we are a city, and have all the hustle and bustle that comes along with it, the little hidden areas are what keep the tourists coming back. The hiking trails, the shopping areas, and our always growing and developing waterfront areas are what help to keep Hamilton on the map. For these reasons, and more, a trip to Hamilton may be one of the best trips you've ever taken.

2. INDUSTRIAL SECTOR

Sure, the Industrial sector doesn't sound fascinating, nor is there much to look at, but because of the Industrial area of Hamilton, the city has been able to flourish as "Steel City". Stelco (currently U.S. Steel Canada) was founded in 1910, and Dominion Foundries and Steel (currently Dofasco) was founded shortly after in 1912. Both companies specialize in the production and manufacturing of multiple types of steel, to be used in multiple types of projects.

The industrial sector, in the North end of Hamilton, might not be much to look at, but depending on how you are entering the city it may very well be the first thing you see. The smoke stacks and freight ships are hard to miss, and actually make up the Hamilton Skyline from the view of Lake Ontario.

Also something that you can generally see, and visit, near the industrial area is the HMCS Haida and the National Historic Site that goes with it. This Tribal Class destroyer actually served in the Second World War, the Korean Conflict, and the Cold war, and is now harbored as a Naval museum in Hamilton.

NEED TO KNOW

3. BEST TIME TO VISIT

As with most tourist destinations, the best time to visit will be when the warmer weather arrives. Typically Hamilton's warmer months are May-September. That being said, we have been known to have unseasonably warm/cold springs and autumns, meaning you could plan a trip earlier or later in the year, but should be prepared for weather changes.

Summer time in Hamilton typically offers the most to do. There are many patios to visit and have a few drinks, and the waterfront viewing is best done in the sun. The trails are dry, and the trees and flowers are in full bloom, offering shade and floral scents on your hike.

Spring would be your ideal time to visit if you're main reason is viewing our waterfalls. Because of the winter thaw, the water tends to be flowing more in March and April, offering a more active view of the waterfalls.

4. VISITING IN AUTUMN

Autumn in Southern Ontario can offer some of the most breathtaking color changes around. While this is a city, a vast majority of the city is covered by trees, which is what makes autumn in Hamilton such a pleasure to see.

There are also a few various farms in the area (Lindley's, and Dyment's) which offer various autumn activities such as corn mazes, pumpkin picking, and various other activities for the kids, and the entire family.

The hiking trails in the fall can also offer some gorgeous views, especially the Bruce trail on the escarpment. This trail will not only give you great hiking views, but also views overlooking the entirety of lower Hamilton.

5. VISITING IN THE WINTER

The winter can be a little more challenging for visiting Hamilton, especially with the unpredictability of the winter weather. If you do choose to venture here during the winter months (November – February), be prepared to take part in some indoor activities, such as the Art Gallery of Hamilton, or some shows at the local theatres.

If you decide that you want to brave the possible cold and have some outdoor fun, then the waterfront could be the place for you. In the winter the bay freezes over and, in certain marked areas, you can actually ice skate right on the water. If you don't have skates, but still want to participate, then I suggest the outdoor rink at Pier 8. Here you can still ice skate outside, but you can rent skates instead of worrying about packing your own!

6. WEATHER

While the running joke is that Canada is always cold, and our Igloos never melt, this is a falsity. I will admit, we do have our cold winters, and sometimes those winters last longer than normal, but generally by May we are steady around 60F or higher. That being said, be sure to bring a jacket, and a sweater with you, as the temperatures can change, even in the summer.

Spending a lot of time in the sun will also cause you to feel colder in the evenings, and a sweater will be your best friend down around the water. In regards to precipitation, we can go days, sometimes weeks without rain, or without sun. It really depends on the weather fronts that are moving through the area. We are too far north to worry about the afternoon storms that some southern parts of the world receive, but rain can still hit us out of nowhere. A windbreaker is suggested, or some other light jacket, and a small umbrella.

7. CURRENCY TO CARRY

Canada has its own currency which we use, meaning your currency will need to be converted beforehand. That being said, some business in Hamilton will accept US currency, however they will accept it the current conversion rate. This means it might actually be cheaper for you to convert your money prior to using it. Converting your money in your place of residence is always encouraged, as you will often get a better rate then you will in a foreign place.

Do not be fooled by our "plastic" money. While most people have spent time laughing at our new currency, we are thoroughly pleased by it. Not only does it look great, but being made out of polymer, they are very hard, if not impossible, to counterfeit, which has cut back on counterfeit currency since their release in 2011.

8. PHRASES TO LEARN

Another popular stereotype of Canadians is that we are insanely polite. Although we are not as polite as some videos and memes will have you believe, we do still take pride in being a polite country. There are no actual phrases you need to worry about learning coming to Hamilton, but your manners would be most welcomed.

If you do happen to hear people talking about things you don't understand, or someone says something with Hamiltonian slang, do not hesitate to ask for clarification. Most of us have no qualms explaining things further. I have thought about a few of the bigger things you may hear. First of all, our largest bridge in Hamilton, leading to Burlington (a city to the North west of us) is called the Skyway bridge. No one ever adds the word bridge, it is just a common knowledge item here. Another thing you will hear a lot is "Tim's" or "Timmies", which is short for Tim Horton's, our main coffee chain here in Canada. Finally you will hear people say "loonie" and "toonie" which are our one dollar, and two dollar coins, respectively.

Other than the above mentioned items there are not many slang terms used by Hamiltonians, or Canadians for that matter, that you will not understand.

9. NEWSPAPERS

There are only two newspapers that you need to concern yourself with while staying in Hamilton, and it depends on what you want to know. For the local news, including the surrounding areas, your best bet will be the Hamilton Spec. This newspaper deals with all news, and is your typical newspaper that you would expect from a city of our size.

For something that deals with more items that may pertain to festivals and events going on you would be best to get a copy of the Hamilton Mountain News. While this mainly deals with news and events that take place on the mountain, it also deals with events in the surrounding areas, which could help if you have a day that you have nothing planned to do!

10. APPS TO DOWNLOAD

While there are not an abundance of apps to concern yourself with in regards to Hamilton, I would suggest downloading the Hamilton Spec, and the Weather Network apps. The Hamilton Spec will give you a digital copy of the newspaper, instead of having to purchase a copy. The Weather Network is our main source for weather information, and is constantly updated, which would be beneficial if your tourist attractions require decent weather.

If you are planning to do some exploring I would also suggest downloading the SoBi app. SoBi, or Social Bicycle, was an initiative put in place a few years ago to cut back on the use of cars. You can add money to your account on the app, and then when you come across the bikes, which are located all around the city, you can type in a code the app will give you, and go riding around the city. You are charged for each 30 minute interval, but you stop being charged when you park and lock the bike! It makes for a fun way to explore the downtown core, and for riding around the bay!

11. WHERE TO STAY

Hamilton is packed with various hotels to stay in, it all depends on where you will be spending most of your time. If you plan on being on the mountain for majority of your trip then I suggest the Marriott Hotel on Upper James. However, if you plan on spending most of your time in the downtown core, or near the water, then The Sheraton Hotel is the place you want to be. The Sheraton is located in the heart of downtown, within walking distance to many local shops and restaurants, Hamilton Place Theatre, and First Ontario Centre.

There are various other hotels sprinkled throughout the city, or you can try your luck with an Air B&B, which could get you closer to the waterfront. If you travel further east in Hamilton you can find various accommodations that are near the beach.

12. TRAVEL

While Hamilton is quite a large city, our airport is not large by any means. The Hamilton International Airport (also known as the John C. Munro airport) is just a short 30 minute drive to downtown Hamilton. The flights coming and going are more of a local nature. If you are visiting from another part of Canada, from the US, or from some Caribbean destinations, then Hamilton International airport should have flights that would be fitting for you.

For more international flights, and for more options, your best bet would be to fly to Pearson Airport (Toronto), which will be a 60 minute drive to the Hamilton downtown core. While it is a further distance, most airports offer an airway taxi which will take you from your airport to your destination for a reasonable price.

13. HOW TO GET AROUND

If you are staying in the downtown core of Hamilton, your best mode of transportation will actually be by foot! Many different areas of the downtown core offer different things to do, and all are generally within walking distance of each other. From the Sheraton Hotel (mentioned above), Bayfront park is only a short 20 minute walk away, for example.

If you are staying in other areas of the city then public transportation via the Hamilton Street Railway (HSR) will be your cheapest option. However, you could also download the Uber app and find drivers that are close by to take you to your destination. The best part about using Uber is that all payments are handled in app. There are always drivers available to take you where you need to go!

If you decide to visit Bayfront park, they also offer a tour bus of sorts, similar to an amusement park shuttle, which will drive you around parts of Bayfront, letting you see everything from the park, to the Yacht Club, and generally stopping around Pier 8.

FOOD SCENE

"Just like becoming an expert in wine – you learn by drinking it, the best you can afford – you learn about great food by finding the best there is, whether simple or luxurious. Then you savor it, analyze it, and discuss it with your companions, and you compare it with other experiences."

Julia Child, Mastering the Art of French Cooking

14. BREAKFAST

If your favorite meal of the day is Breakfast, like myself, then Hamilton offers you some amazing places to eat! It really all depends on what you are in the mood for, and where you are located. First on the list is Cora's, which is a franchised business that originated in Quebec. They offer a wide variety of your usual breakfast food options, however all of their dishes come with a large portion of freshly cut fruit, that they prepare daily.

If you're looking for something that isn't a franchise, then you would be best to visit The Egg and I. They have two locations to choose from, and if you are staying on Upper James I would highly recommend them. They have delicious food, and great prices. If you're staying near the downtown core then I would suggest visiting the Harbor Front Diner. They also have a wide variety of breakfast options, but they specialize in a Lobster Benny (egg's benedict with lobster). It is amazing!

Finally, if you are staying closer to the east end of the city then The Bedrock Bistro is the place for you. This Flintstone's themed restaurant offers all day breakfast, and they also have some delicious options.

15. LUNCH

Perhaps breakfast is the meal that you usually skip, but lunch is where you meet your hunger head on. In that case why not chow down on some delicious, but lighter food, in the Locke Street and downtown core area. One place to eat, which has amazing food, is Democracy on Locke. This restaurant has a large menu, for fair prices, and everything on it is completely Vegan! As someone who is not Vegan, I can say from experience that their food is incredible, regardless of your food preference.

You could also hit a few different walk in places along King Street such as Bastoni's (specializing in Shawarma, and Shawarma poutine – you have to try it), or even the restaurants in Hess village (off of King Street). The places on Hess have amazing food, but beware on the weekends after about 8pm; Hess is the night club street, and the place to be for many of the younger inhabitants of the city.

16. DINNER

For dinner, why not hit up a few delicious Pub's and grab some amazing food and a pint! One place you have to visit is Augusta street. There are a variety of different pubs here that have a great selection of beer on tap, and have an amazing menu. A few I would suggest are Gallagher's Bar & Lounge, The Ship, and Aout 'N About.

If you're looking for a different experience, then you should try The Black Forest Inn, which specializes in German cuisine. Locke Street also has some great places to visit, such as Brux House Craft Beer & Kitchen, Beasley House Bistro, and Mattson & Co. All offer a great menu, and an even nicer drink menu!

17. DRINKS

After dinner, or during the afternoon, if you're looking for a great place to grab a drink, Hamilton has a lot of different places to choose from. The first place to mention is Augusta Street, where you can participate in a Pub Crawl during certain times of the year, or create one yourself! There are a variety of different pubs to choose from, or you can visit them all!

Another place to grab a few drinks would be Hess Village. Again, after 8pm on the weekend the clubs open up, and this place is crowded with a younger crowd, but during the day these restaurants offer great food, and even better drinks!

There are also a few places on Locke Street which provide some amazing patio's to sit on while enjoying your beverage! Some places were already mentioned above, but a few others include The Beverly on Locke, and West Town Bar & Grill.

18. SNACKS AND DESSERTS

The snack scene in Hamilton is where it is at! You can get so many delicious things, from so many delicious places all throughout the city. Many of the items are baked goods, but who doesn't love baked goods.

The first place to mention is on Locke Street. If you have a chance then you need to visit Donut Monster, where they specialize in some amazing donuts, with some very interesting flavors, such as their Carrot and Pineapple Fritter, Sriracha Lime, and even Mexican Chocolate. Their donuts are amazing, and quite large! Also on Locke is Bitten. This bakery specializes in cupcakes and whoopie pies, and they are incredible!

Another place to check out is the Cake & Loaf Bakery on Dundurn Street. They also offer some amazing and delicious items including cakes, pies, and pastries, as well as cupcakes! Finally, my own business, Confectionary Creations, offers some delicious vegan baked goods, at a regular price point. While we don't currently have a stand-alone shop, you can always place an order when you're in town!

19. COFFEE AND TEA

For those who have a slight caffeine addiction, and require a delicious cup of coffee to start the day, continue the day, or just because, then Hamilton has an amazing café experience for you.

Whether you are looking for a cozy coffee shop to spend your afternoon in, or a gorgeous patio to people watch, the choices are endless.

One of my favorite places to visit is Café Oranje. This Dutch-inspired coffee shop, boasts a brilliant variety of coffees and coffee beverages, and offers amazing food pairings to go with it. Their rustic theme is quite amazing as well.

Another shop to visit would be My Dog Joe in Westdale Village. This is the coffee shop for the students at McMaster University, but the service is fairly quick and their coffee is strong and delicious!

Democracy is another one I would suggest as well. As mentioned above they specialize in Vegan food, but their coffee game is also on point! To top it off they have some pretty amazing goodies to pair with your coffee, and when the weather is just right they open their front window wide for an open concept experience that can't be beat.

20. STREET FOOD

While many cities boast about their various street food vendors, in Hamilton our food scene, especially our street food, is unbeatable. While we may not have the falafel carts, or the street meat vendors, we have a wide variety of food trucks that you can find all through the city.

If you choose to visit during certain festivals or events in the city, then most locations generally have a few food trucks and vendors ready to go. A few that you need to try are Gorilla Cheese, Curbside Burgers, and Green Machine.

Gorilla Cheese was actually featured on an episode of Dragon's Den, and the sandwiches they were serving blew the minds of the judges. One of my personal favourites is The Lumberjack, which has granny smith apples, maple syrup, and cheese! They do have a lot of other options, and their prices are great!

For something that will appeal to the more health conscious individual, The Green Machine is the best bet for you. They have some healthy alternatives with their fresh smoothies and juices, which are out of this world! Finally, if you're looking for something a little more "normal" we suggest Curbside Burgers for some absolutely delicious burgers and fries! They have loads of toppings, and their burgers are cooked to perfection!

ENTERTAINMENT

"My philosophy is: if you can't have fun, there's no sense in doing it."

Paul Walker

21. NIGHT LIFE

The night life in Hamilton is quite exciting, but very age dependent. If you are a younger individual (19-25) you would be better suited to visit Hess Village between Thursday and Saturday. The village becomes the night club haven during the summer months, and well into autumn. There are many to choose from, depending on your music taste and your intentions. If you are looking for more of a dance club then Sizzle and Koi are the clubs for you. They blast amazing beats and you can arrange bottle service for you and your friends while you are there. If you are looking for something that is a little more laid back then I suggest Gown and Gavel. While they still play your dance beats, the atmosphere is very different.

If you are over the age of 25 then perhaps you would be more interested in the Pub scene that Hamilton has to offer. If this is the case then Augusta Street is the place to be. With a dozen pubs within walking distance of each other, you will be able to find something that suits you just fine. A few to mention are The Ship, The Pheasant Plucker, Gallagher's, and The Cat 'n' Fiddle. All of these pubs offer a variety of beer, both domestic and craft, on tap. They also all offer some amazing pub food!

22. THEATRE LIFE

With a few different theatres in Hamilton, perhaps you might take in a show while you are here. The Staircase Theatre, Hamilton Theatre, and Theatre Aquarius all have some amazing shows that go on year round. It really all depends on your taste.

Some of the musicals that are put on in Theatre Aquarius are quite entertaining. I have had the pleasure to see a few shows in this theatre and they give you a very professional quality performance!

The Hamilton Theatre company also offers you some very good performances. The venues for this company can change, but the quality of the shows do not. They offer a more minimalistic performance, in regards to staging, but for what they lack in big, complicated sets, they make up for with raw talent!

The Staircase Theatre offers you a different kind of experience. While both the Hamilton Theatre Company, and Theatre Aquarius offer you more than just musicals, The Staircase theatre delves into some deeper stage productions. They have played some intriguing, macabre, and hilarious performances throughout the years, and always leave the audience craving another performance.

23. FILM INDUSTRY

Hamilton, with all of its small town charm in a big city setting, has been lucky to be the back drop for many blockbuster films throughout the years. Some iconic scenes have been filmed in some of our most remote locations, which are easily recognizable. Some of the films that have utilized Hamilton's beauty are Silent Hill, The Incredible Hulk, and even X-Men.

In addition to these films Hamilton has been the setting for a few different episodes of a different shows. Hemlock Grove on Netflix filmed many of their scenes here in Hamilton and Toronto, as did Murdoch Mysteries.

Nominated for numerous academy awards in 2017, The Shape of Water was filmed here in Hamilton, and in the surrounding cities as well.

24. MUSIC SCENE

The music scene in Hamilton may not be as large as it sounds, but we are constantly home to many different musicians and bands. We have been proud to host the Juno's, Canada's music awards, and the Canadian Country Music Awards as well.

The various Pubs in Hamilton are always showcasing new talent from the city, and these live shows are amazing to watch. In many cases this is how new musicians get their name out there and gain a following.

One such band, from Hamilton, is The Arkells. They are known for their Alternative Rock style and catchy lyrics. They are very big on getting the crowds that they play for into the music! Starting out in Hamilton they have debuted at Coachella, Lollapalooza, and Bonnaroo, and they show no signs of slowing down. They stay true to their roots, with many of their songs having a Hamilton vibe!

25. ARTS SCENE

Hamilton has one of the largest art scenes in the area, and has many street festivals to prove it. If you have the privilege of being in Hamilton in early September then you will be able to take in everything that Super Crawl has to offer. This street fest shuts down most of James Street, allowing vendors to set up shop to showcase and sell their art. Food trucks come out, and there are many live concerts being performed, with Super Crawl occurring for an entire weekend.

If you are unable to attend Super Crawl, there is no need to worry. On the second Friday of every month, James Street is transformed into something known as Art Crawl, which is essentially Super Crawl on a smaller scale. You will still be able to visit all of the vendors and studios, but the live music and food trucks may or may not be present.

26. FESTIVALS - HAMILTON

There are a wide variety of Festivals that occur throughout most of the summer and autumn in Hamilton. The best festivals to take part in are the Festival of Friends, It's Your Festival, and the Apple Festival.

The Festival of Friends is an annual, three day, music festival that occurs in the summer months at Gage Park. The admission for the festival is free, and there are lots of vendors and activities to take part in. With the George R. Robinson Bandshell in the park the music that is played can be heard throughout the area, offering the crowds a great experience regardless of their location.

It's Your Festival occurs near the end of June, and is put on by the Hamilton Folk Arts Heritage Council. The festival is a great place to come out and take part, and learn about, our local heritage. There are various vendors, as well as a Food's from Around the World section, where you can taste some delicious food items from lots of different locals. This festival also takes place in Gage Park.

The Apple Festival occurs in mid to late September, at our historic Battlefield Park. The festival has free admission (regular admission rates apply to the museum) and offers a pancake breakfast, games, pumpkin decorating, demonstrations, and entertainment. The workers at the festivals are all in period clothing from the 1800's, which makes the event a very unique experience.

27. FESTIVALS - NEARBY

If you are able to travel outside of the city, then there are three festivals that cannot be missed. The Dundas Cactus festival is something that is incredible, especially given that it began because of the Ben Veldhuis Cactus Greenhouses, which were producing Cacti that are internationally recognized. The Cactus fest is located on King Street in Dundas, about a 15 minute drive from Downtown Hamilton. You will find vendors, amazing entertainment, activities for the kids, and some great food!

If you are in Hamilton in June make sure that you head over to Burlington and experience The Sound of Music Festival. While some concerts may cost you a small fee, most of the festival is completely free, and the music is amazing. There are lots of vendors, a midway, amazing food, and lots of live music on 4-5 various stages throughout the Spencer Smith Park.

About half an hour away from Downtown Hamilton, is the small town of Winona. This town, though small, fills up fast in August, where everyone heads to the Winona Peach Festival. Like most of the festivals there are loads of vendors, amazing food, and lots of entertainment. What keeps me going back each year is their delicious peach sundaes, and baskets of fresh peaches. Shuttles are usually available from various locations in Hamilton, which means you have no excuse not to visit this amazing festival!

FOR THE KIDS

"You're off to great places,
today is your day! Your mountain is
waiting, so get on your way!"

Dr. Seuss

28. WILD WATER WORKS

If you are looking for something that you can bring the kids to for a fun day in the sun, then Wild Water Works is the place to be. Open all summer long, and located down near the Hamilton Beach, Wild Water Works, also known as Confederation Park, offers a lot of fun, and is very affordable.

With one of the largest outdoor wave pools in Canada, you can swim o your hearts content, or float around in a rental tube. You can also enjoy 6 unique waterslides, some using inner tubes, some without. If you want to just lounge and relax, you can always float around the lazy river!

If you have younger kids with you they also offer a kid sized splash area, which also offers some water slides for them as well! Pack yourself a picnic lunch as this park allows you to bring in your own food and drinks (alcohol not permitted), giving you the chance to have a great and affordable day out with the kids!

29. ADVENTURE VILLAGE

If you finish at Wild Water Works and are still looking for something to do, then a few minutes down the road is Adventure Village. Here you can partake in the arcade, or enjoy some of their other unique experiences. They have rock climbing, outdoor laser tag, bungee trampolines, and gemstone mining.

If you want something a little more laid back you can also play a wonderful game of Mini Golf, or let the kids race around on the Go Karts. For those athletic families looking for something to do, Adventure Village also has Batting Cages!

30. AFRICAN LION SAFARI

Half an hours outside of Hamilton, is our very own Safari! The African Lion Safari is "Canada's Original

Safari Adventure", where you can come face to face with exotic birds and animals.

At the African Lion Safari you can walk around and visit the various enclosures to see some of these incredible animals up close and personal. However if you are looking for something even better, you can take part in a safari in your own vehicle. You drive through some various locations getting a closer look at the monkeys, the giraffes, and even the pride of lions. If you would like something a little more interactive you can also hop aboard the African Queen and partake in a boat cruise around the park.

Make sure to bring your bathing suit, as African Lion Safari offers a wet play area known as Misumu Bay!

31. CHERRY HILL GATE

Part of Hamilton's Royal Botanical Garden (RBG) area, is Cherry Hill Gate. While this may be considered a hiking trail of sorts, it is something that you will want to bring your kids to! I will start by encouraging you to bring bird seed, sunflower seeds, and perhaps even some peanuts. The wildlife in this area is amazing, and because of the regular foot traffic of people, the animals have become accustomed to our presence and do not run away in fear. The squirrels and chipmunks will come up and eat the food right out of your hands, and on the boardwalk surrounding the wetlands you can hold your hand out and have a variety of birds land for a feast of seed!

If you look down over the boardwalk, and into the marshlands you can see muskrats, swans, Canadian geese, ducks, and even some various fish! There are dams sprinkled all through the marsh, and if you're lucky you may even catch a glimpse of a beaver!

LOCAL

32. SCHOOLS

Perhaps you are visiting Hamilton with anticipation of coming to the city for Education, and if that's the case, you've picked a great city. Hamilton is home to three Post-Secondary Educational institutions: Mohawk College, McMaster University, and Brock University (Hamilton Campus).

Mohawk College is an amazing school, offering a wide variety of programs in many different fields. Most of their programs come in different styles, with each taking a different length of time. For example, if you are interested in Architecture, you have two options to choose from. The first is Architectural Technician, which offers you all of the courses required to complete your diploma program in 2 years. The second is Architectural Technology, which will offer you similar courses, but will also offer you two working periods in which you are required to find a paid co-op position for 2 semesters, making it a 3 year program. Most of the programs at Mohawk have a co-op option, which is great for those who want hands on experience in their field, pre-graduation.

McMaster University is Hamilton's main university. They also offer a wide variety of programs and degrees, but are mainly associate with Arts, Engineering, and Medical degrees. The campus is quite large, and is always being update, making it a very modern and beautiful school and campus.

Finally, the Brock University Hamilton campus, is located on King Street in downtown Hamilton. While the main campus is located in St. Catherine's, 45 minutes away, the Hamilton campus is utilized as the Teacher's college, where individuals can complete their Bachelor's Degree in Education. While some travel to and from the St. Catherine's campus may be necessary, it is nice to boast about 3 educational institutes in our lovely city.

33. HOLIDAYS

Depending on the time of your visit, you may run into some various Holiday's that you were not anticipating. While we celebrate all the traditional Holiday's such as New Years, Christmas, and Easter, Canada has a few Holiday's of their own.

If you are visiting around May 24, then you will be here for all of our Victoria Day celebrations. The weekend of May 24th is a long weekend for many business and schools, and many things are often closed on the 24th in order to celebrate the birthday of Queen Victoria.

If you end up visiting around July 1st, then you may be celebrating Canada Day with us. Much like Independence Day in America, Canada Day is when we celebrate becoming a single Dominion within the British Empire. Most stores and businesses will be closed during this day.

In both cases you will be able to find many different areas in the city celebrating with gorgeous fireworks displays, which gives you something to do during the Holiday, and something to look forward to!

HISTORY

"If you don't know history, then you don't know anything. You are a leaf that doesn't know it is part of a tree."

Michael Crichton

34. TIM HORTON'S

In 1964 two Hamilton hockey players, and soon to be business partners, ventured into the world of hamburger restaurants, which fizzled out fast. These partners, Jim Charade and Tim Horton, eventually opened the first Tim Horton's location on Ottawa Street in Hamilton, and partnered with investor Ron

Joyce, who took over operations when Horton died in 1974.

Tim Horton's has been, and always will be, a Canadian staple, and with its origins in Hamilton, you can understand why we are so patriotic towards this coffee company. Their coffee is delicious, and their other treats are amazing as well. Although you will see one on almost every street in Hamilton, the original location on Ottawa Street has been updated and renovated and is a great place to visit to learn about the history of the company!

35. DUNDURN CASTLE

Dundurn Castle, located on York Boulevard in Hamilton, overlooks the Burlington Heights (present day Dundurn Park), and was constructed in 1835. Sir Allen MacNab, who was the Premier of the United Province of Canada between 1954 and 1956, hired the architect, Richard Beasley, to complete the building in 1935.

Dundurn Castle, once completed, was famous all over the country due to its grand entertainments, and was visited by Sir John A. Macdonald, and King

Edward VII. In 1855 other adornments were added to the castle as part of the wedding preparations for Sophia, MacNab's daughter.

The castle and grounds are now open to the public as part of a museum experience, where guests can take in what the castle would have been like in the 1800's. Historically speaking, the grounds have been the home of various historic events throughout the years, including a mass hanging years prior to the construction of the castle. During the War of 1812, nine men were found guilty and convicted of treason, and were hanged at the eastern end of Dundurn park.

There are numerous other parts of Dundurn castle, including its very own folly, which is rumored to be the entrance to one of many underground tunnels leading to and from the main castle.

36. BATTLEFIELD PARK

On June 6, 1813, the British units, stationed in Stoney Creek, Ontario, made a night attack on an American encampment. The Americans, having under estimated the strength of the British forces, had two of their senior officers captured and the battle was a victory for the British. This battle, part of the War of 1812, was part of the reason for the erecting of the Battlefield Park monument, and the opening of the park as a memorial to those who fought in the War.

The corner stone of the monument, with all funds being collected by the Women's Wentworth historical Society and the Wentworth Historical Society, was laid on May 26, 1910, and the monument was unveiled by Queen Mary, in London (by means of transatlantic cable) on June 6, 1913; the centennial anniversary of the battle.

The monument still stands today, and the surrounding park and museum serves as a place for people to learn about Hamilton's history in the War of 1812. The monument also offers a unique experience where you can see how certain jobs and crafts would have been completed in the 1800's, complete with period clothing. If you have a chance to visit, especially around June 6th, I would suggest it. They recreate the battle of Stoney Creek and it is always something amazing to see!

37. FOOTBALL HALL OF FAME AND THE HAMILTON TIGER CATS

If you are a sports fan, and more importantly, a Football fan, than the Canadian Football Hall of Fame (CFHOF) may be something that is right up your alley. Located in downtown Hamilton is the CFHOF, offering a lot of various memorabilia and moments in Canadian Football League (CFL) history.

While you are here, and if you have a chance, you should take in a home game for the Hamilton Tiger Cats. Down at Tim Horton's Field you can watch the Tiger Cats "Eat 'em Raw", and take part in a Hamilton tradition.

The Hamilton Tiger Cats, our official CFL team, were founded in 1950 when our two teams, The Hamilton Tigers, and The Hamilton Wildcats, merged. Since then they have won the Grey Cup championship 8 times, the most recent being in 1999.

PHOTO OP'S

"Photography for me is not looking, it's feeling. If you can't feel what you're looking at, then you're never going to get others to feel anything when they look at your pictures."

Don McCullin

38. DEVIL'S PUNCHBOWL

Although the name may suggest a very creepy place, The Devil's Punchbowl is actually an amazing lookout spot for the entire downtown city of Hamilton/Stoney Creek.

There are many stories as to how the area got its name, but the most popular is that Moonshiners lived in the area, and would travel to the base of the falls to get cold water. Because they were doing the "Devil's work", the place was nicknamed the Devil's Punchbowl, and that has remained its name ever since.

51

If you are traveling up the escarpment, or are downtown looking in the direction of the punchbowl at night, you may notice a large illuminated cross overlooking the cliff. This cross was put up in 1966 with the intention on only being lit during Christmas and Easter. Because of donations, the cross lights up each night.

The water fall that drains into the center of the punchbowl has a 108 foot drop, and has been the backdrop for a few different movies, Silent Hill (2006) included.

39. HIKING TRAILS

Hamilton has many various hiking trails that you can choose from, and many other trails within driving distance. Perhaps one of the most used trails is the Bruce Trail. While the Bruce trail is not necessarily a Hamilton trail, it does wind the entirety of the Hamilton escarpment, and offers some amazing views of the city.

The Bruce Trail is actually a trail that stretches from Niagara Falls all the way to the Bruce Peninsula (a 6 hour drive by car). Some people have hiked this and say that the views all along the trail are magnificent. I can only speak for the Hamilton portion of the trail, and if you are into hiking, you cannot pass up the opportunity.

There are many other wooded areas around the outskirts of Hamilton, which offer you other hiking trails to partake in, but most of them will eventually run into the Bruce trail at some point!

40. ERAMOSA KARST

The Eramosa Karst, located on the Hamilton East Mountain, is one of Hamilton's, and Ontario's, best examples of karstic topography. Whether you are looking to explore caves, go for a hike, or sightsee, this is a destination you will want to check out.

While wandering along the hiking trails you can peer into karst windows, which occur when the tops of caves collapse in, leaving you a window to peer through. There are a few of these spread out through the trails, and a map that you receive at the beginning of the hike will help you locate them all.

There is also a cave entrance, known as the Nexus cave, which is located halfway through your hike, which actually offers brave souls the chance to get down into the cave. There are no guides along this walk, so you enter any cave at your own risk. The temperature shift is also something you need to anticipate, and be prepared for, so long sleeves are suggested.

41. NIAGARA ESCARPMENT

The Hamilton escarpment, which separates the mountain from lower Hamilton, is actually part of a bigger escarpment, known as the Niagara escarpment. This escarpment, runs from New York, thorough Ontario, Michigan, Wisconsin, and Illinois, and is most famous for where the Niagara River drops off at Niagara Falls, Ontario.

In Hamilton you will find the Bruce Trail, a hiking trail, carved into the escarpment, offering you a way to see the city like no other. However, if you choose to venture outside of Hamilton there are many other parts of the escarpment that you can see. Rattlesnake Point, Mt. Nemo, and even places closer to Niagara falls, allow you some breathtaking views, and some amazing trails.

The escarpment is a United Nations Educational, Scientific and Cultural Organization (UNESCO) World Biosphere reserve, and has the oldest forest ecosystem in all of North America.

WATERFRONT

"What I love most about rivers is, you can't step in the same river twice; the water's always changing, always flowing. But people I guess can't live like that, we all must pay a price; to be safe we lose our chance of ever knowing."

Pocahontas

42. WATERFALLS

Hamilton is known as the waterfall capital of the world, due to the number of waterfalls that we have within our city limits. This is due to us being a large part of the Niagara Escarpment, which gives us 100 natural waterfalls within the city. While some of the waterfalls are not overly large, some of them are quite gorgeous, and offer a great place to cool off and enjoy the view.

If you are strapped for time and can only visit a few of the waterfalls, there are a few that shouldn't be missed. The first is Mount Albion Falls, located along Upper Mount Albion Road. If you choose to do so you can also access these falls by hiking through some of the Bruce trail, leading you to the base of the falls. By being at the base, you an actually get into the down pour and take some wonderful pictures, as other tourists have.

Another area you should put on your list is Tiffany Falls. These falls are located just off of Wilson Street in Ancaster, and have a tiered waterfall system, offering a unique view.

Of course, if you are able to and have the time, I suggest visiting as many as you can, and take a picture at each location. Each one is unique in its own way, and each location offers you something new as well.

43. BAYFRONT PARK AND PIER 4

If the Hamilton waterfront is something that you want to take in, and you should, then Bayfront Park and Pier 4 is one place that you will need to visit. Bayfront park is a small land formation in the Hamilton harbor, that offers amazing views of the water, and is perfect for a day out walking the trails, biking, roller blading, or just lounging around.

If you want a lengthier walk, and more views, you can actually walk a long path alongside the railroad tracks, which will take you to the lookout for Coote's Paradise, a small inlet that the Hamilton harbor runs into.

Or, if you would like to bring the kids to look at some of the sailing vessels, walking over to Pier 4 will be your best option. Near Pier 4 you have a small splash pad and tug boat park that the kids can play at, and you can view all of the boats, most of which belong to the Royal Hamilton Yacht Club (RHYC), which is located at Pier 4.

44. THE HAMILTON BEACH STRIP

The Hamilton Beach Strip might be the best place to just sit and stare at the water and completely relax. The water itself is rather cold, and the beach is a swim at your own risk beach, meaning swimming may not always be an option, but it is still a place you need to visit.

You can walk along the beach path and look at all of the amazing architecture of the beach homes in the area, or take in a beach volley ball game down near Barangas, an amazing little restaurant.

If you continue walking down the path you will eventually come across Adventure Village, mentioned earlier, giving you and your kids some fun things to do while you are down there.

If you do make your way to the beach strip, one place you need to visit is Hutches on the Beach. This little restaurant has been around since 1946 and is famous for their delicious Fish and Chip meals. You can also enjoy some ice cream, as they have tons of flavors to choose from.

PLACES TO WALK

"A city building, you experience when you walk; a suburban building, you experience when you drive."
Helmut Jahn

45. LOCKE STREET

Locke Street, as mentioned in previous sections, boasts some incredible dining experiences, but there is so much more to Locke Street than food. While on Locke street be sure to stop in at the various shops along the way. The book stores, the tea shops, and the various antique shops cannot be seen anywhere else, and as such, should be taken in!

In September the Locke Street Festival is something to take in! The entire street is shut down, and only foot traffic is allowed for the day. There are lots of various vendors that come out, and the shops are all open as well. There is lots of entertainment, and live music, and the food scene is incredible.

46. OTTAWA STREET

A street that has yet to be mentioned is Ottawa Street, which is a street that showcases the eclectic spirit of Hamilton. There are over 100 shops to find here, which features some incredible fashion finds, and some amazing food.

On this street you can find a lot of various boutiques and fashion shops, as well as various textile shops. Much like Locke Street there are also lots of various galleries, bookshops, and antique shops that have some unique items to offer. The food on this street is incredible. I mentioned the Gorilla Cheese food truck earlier, and on Ottawa Street you can visit their new shop, to enjoy some delicious food!

47. JAMES STREET

Whether you are visiting with the intent on taking part in art crawl or supercrawl, James Street is not something you can pass up on. This street has some unique food experiences, and also has some incredible shops and art galleries, that can't be missed. Like the other walking areas, James Street is around six or seven blocks, but it will take you a few hours to visit and take in everything it has to offer.

If you end up being in the area on the second Friday of the month, and you visit during the day, make sure to return at night. Some of the galleries rent out additional space to other artists and exhibits, and the streets are often loaded with vendors selling lots of other unique items that you will not find anywhere else.

48. INTERNATIONAL VILLAGE

In the heart of Hamilton's' downtown core is an area known by most as International Village. This stretch of King Street offers some amazing shops and areas to eat, and lives up to its name. Here you will find shops that sell a wide variety of items, with each shop specializing in a different place from around the world. The food down here has the same trend, with everything from East Indian food, to Greek, and even some Chinese food areas as well.

While International Village is only around five or six blocks, it will take you most of an afternoon to visit everything and take it all in. Luckily, this area is one of the nicest areas to walk around, and offers lots of shade to keep you cool in the summer!

49. SAFETY AND SECURITY

Much like any big city, there are always places that you should avoid at certain times. Hamilton is no exception to this rule. While you should be perfectly safe at all hours, just expect a different crowd to be around after midnight. Hamilton does have a large homeless population, and most of them will be walking around after dark, looking for a place to sleep, or for food.

There also isn't much to do in the city after dark, other than areas mentioned in the entertainment section. If you feel compelled to walk around at night, a cliché term that applies is "safety in numbers". Feel free to explore, but be smart and use your head.

50. SOUVENIRS TO BUY

There are not a whole lot of souvenirs to purchase in regards to Hamilton, but there are a lot of places that sell loads of Canada items. If this is what you are after then I suggest visiting The Bay in Limeridge Mall. They are the official carriers of all Team Canada items, which includes clothing, bags, and accessories.

If a Hamilton souvenir is what you have your heart set on than I suggest visiting True Hamiltonian. This store is open on Melrose Avenue and there is also a shop in Limeridge Mall. They specialize in clothing that shows Hamilton pride, with their main logo being "Hamilton is Home".

TOP REASONS TO BOOK THIS TRIP

Waterfront: With Bayfront, Pier 8, Pier 4, the Hamilton Beach, and more waterfalls than I can count, our waterfront is better than any!

Food: Whether you are looking at the local restaurants, the pubs, or even the food trucks, there is something here that you won't find anywhere else!

History: Our city is loaded with History. From the war of 1812, to the beginnings of a nationwide franchise, we have lots to boast about.

BONUS BOOK

50 THINGS TO KNOW ABOUT PACKING LIGHT FOR TRAVEL

PACK THE RIGHT WAY EVERY TIME

AUTHOR: MANIDIPA BHATTACHARYYA

Edited by Melanie Howthorne

ABOUT THE AUTHOR

Manidipa Bhattacharyya is a creative writer and editor, with an education in English literature and Linguistics. After working in the IT industry for seven long years she decided to call it quits and follow her heart instead. Manidipa has been ghost writing, editing, proof reading and doing secondary research services for many story tellers and article writers for about three years. She stays in Kolkata, India with her husband and a busy two year old. In her own time Manidipa enjoys travelling, photography and writing flash fiction.

Manidipa believes in travelling light and never carries anything that she couldn't haul herself on a trip. However, travelling with her child changed the scenario. She seemed to carry the entire world with her for the baby on the first two trips. But good sense prevailed and she is again working her way to becoming a light traveler, this time with a kid.

INTRODUCTION

He who would travel happily
must travel light.

-Antoine de Saint-Exupéry

Travel takes you to different places from seas and mountains to deserts and much more. In your travels you get to interact with different people and their cultures. You will, however, enjoy the sights and interact positively with these new people even more, if you are travelling light.

When you travel light your mind can be free from worry about your belongings. You do not have to spend precious vacation time waiting for your luggage to arrive after a long flight. There is be no chance of your bags going missing and the best part is that you need not pay a fee for checked baggage.

People who have mastered this art of packing light will root for you to take only one carry-on, wherever you go. However, many people can find it really hard to pack light. More so if you are travelling with children. Differentiating between "must have" and "just in case" items is the starting point. There will be ample shopping avenues at your destination which are just waiting to be explored.

69

This book will show you 'packing' in a new 'light' –
pun intended – and help you to embrace light
packing practices for all of your future travels.

Off to packing!

DEDICATION

I dedicate this book to all the travel buffs that I know,
who have given me great insights into the contents of
their backpacks.

THE RIGHT TRAVEL GEAR

1. CHOOSE YOUR TRAVEL GEAR CAREFULLY

While selecting your travel gear, pick items that are
light weight, durable and most importantly, easy to
carry. There are cases with wheels so you can drag
them along – these are usually on the heavy side
because of the trolley. Alternatively a backpack that
you can carry comfortably on your back, or even a
duffel bag that you can carry easily by hand or sling
across your body are also great options. Whatever
you choose, one thing to keep in mind is that the
luggage itself should not weigh a ton, this will give
you the flexibility to bring along one extra pair of
shoes if you so desire.

2. CARRY THE MINIMUM NUMBER OF BAGS

Selecting light weight luggage is not everything. You need to restrict the number of bags you carry as well. One carry-on size bag is ideal for light travel. Most carriers allow one cabin baggage plus one purse, handbag or camera bag as long as it slides under the seat in front. So technically, you can carry two items of luggage without checking them in.

3. PACK ONE EXTRA BAG

Always pack one extra empty bag along with your essential items. This could be a very light weight duffel bag or even a sturdy tote bag which takes up minimal space. In the event that you end up buying a lot of souvenirs, you already have a handy bag to stuff all that into and do not have to spend time hunting for an appropriate bag.

I'm very strict with my packing and have everything in its right place. I never change a rule. I hardly use anything in the hotel room. I wheel my own wardrobe in and that's it.

Charlie Watts

CLOTHES & ACCESSORIES

4. PLAN AHEAD

Figure out in advance what you plan to do on your trip. That will help you to pick that one dress you need for the occasion. If you are going to attend a wedding then you have to carry formal wear. If not, you can ditch the gown for something lighter that will be comfortable during long walks or on the beach.

5. WEAR THAT JACKET

Remember that wearing items will not add extra luggage for your air travel. So wear that bulky jacket that you plan to carry for your trip. This saves space and can also help keep you warm during the chilly flight.

6. MIX AND MATCH

Carry clothes that can be interchangeably used to reinvent your look. Find one top that goes well with a couple of pairs of pants or skirts. Use tops, shirts and jackets wisely along with other accessories like a scarf or a stole to create a new look.

7. CHOOSE YOUR FABRIC WISELY

Stuffing clothes in cramped bags definitely takes its toll which results in wrinkles. It is best to carry wrinkle free, synthetic clothes or merino tops. This will eliminate the need for that small iron you usually bring along.

8. DITCH CLOTHES PACK UNDERWEAR

Pack more underwear and socks. These are the things that will give you a fresh feel even if you do not get a chance to wear fresh clothes. Moreover these are easy to wash and can be dried inside the hotel room itself.

9. CHOOSE DARK OVER LIGHT

While picking your clothes choose dark coloured ones. They are easy to colour coordinate and can last longer before needing a wash. Accidental food spills and dirt from the road are less visible on darker clothes.

10. WEAR YOUR JEANS

Take only one pair of Jeans with you, which you should wear on the flight. Remember to pick a pair that can be worn for sightseeing trips and is equally eloquent for dinner. You can add variety by adding light weight cargoes and chinos.

11. CARRY SMART ACCESSORIES

The right accessory can give you a fresh look even with the same old dress. An intelligent neck-piece, a couple of bright scarves, stoles or a sarong can be used in a number of ways to add variety to your clothing. These light weight beauties can double up as a nursing cover, a light blanket, beach wear, a modesty cover for visiting places of worship, and also makes for an enthralling game of peek-a-boo.

12. LEARN TO FOLD YOUR GARMENTS

Seasoned travellers all swear by rolling their clothes for compact and wrinkle free packing. Bundle packing, where you roll the clothes around a central object as if tying it up, is also a popular method of compact and wrinkle free packing. Stacking folded clothes one on top of another is a big no-no as it makes creases extreme and they are difficult to get rid of without ironing.

13. WASH YOUR DIRTY LAUNDRY

One of the ways to avoid carrying loads of clothes is to wash the clothes you carry. At some places you might get to use the laundry services or a Laundromat but if you are in a pinch, best solution is to wash them yourself. If that is the plan then carrying quick drying clothes is highly recommended, which most often also happen to be the wrinkle free variety.

14. LEAVE THOSE TOWELS BEHIND

Regular towels take up a lot of space, are heavy and take ages to dry out. If you are staying at hotels they will provide you with towels anyway. If you are travelling to a remote place, where the availability of towels look doubtful, carry a light weight travel towel of viscose material to do the job.

15. USE A COMPRESSION BAG

Compression bags are getting lots of recommendation now days from regular travellers. These are useful for saving space in your luggage when you have to pack bulky dresses. While packing for the return trip, get help from the hotel staff to arrange a vacuum cleaner.

FOOTWEAR

16. PUT ON YOUR HIKING BOOTS

If you have plans to go hiking or trekking during your trip, you will need those bulky hiking boots. The best way to carry them is to wear them on flight to save space and luggage weight. You can remove the boots once inside and be comfortable in your socks.

17. PICKING THE RIGHT SHOES

Shoes are often the bulkiest items, along with being the dainty if you are a female. They need care and take up a lot of space in your luggage. It is advisable therefore to pick shoes very carefully. If you plan to do a lot of walking and site seeing, then wearing a pair of comfortable walking shoes are a must. For more formal occasions you can carry durable, light weight flats which will not take up much space.

18. STUFF SHOES

If you happen to pack a pair of shoes, ensure you utilize their hollow insides. Tuck small items like rolled up socks or belts to save space. They will also be easy to find.

TOILETRIES

19. STASHING TOILETRIES

Carry only absolute necessities. Airline rules dictate that for one carry-on bag, liquids and gels must be in 3.4 ounce (100ml) bottles or less, and must be packed in a one quart zip-lock bag. If you are planning to stay in a hotel, the basic things will be provided for you. It's best is to buy the rest from the local market at your destination.

20. TAKE ALONG TAMPONS

Tampons are a hard to find item in a lot of countries. Figure out how many you need and pack accordingly. For longer stays you can buy them online and have them delivered to where you are staying.

21. GET PAMPERED BEFORE YOU TRAVEL

Some avid travellers suggest getting a pedicure and manicure just the day before travelling. This not only gives you a well kept look, you also save the trouble of packing nail polish. Remember, every little bit of weight reduced adds up.

ELECTRONICS
22. LUGGING ALONG ELECTRONICS

Electronics have a large role to play in our lives today. Most of us cannot imagine our lives away from our phones, laptops or tablets. However while travelling, one must consider the amount of weight these electronics add to our luggage. Thankfully smart phones come along with all the essentials tools like a camera, email access, picture editing tools and more. They are smart to the point of eliminating the need to carry multiple gadgets. Choose a smart phone that suits all your requirements and travel with the world in your palms or pocket.

23. REDUCE THE NUMBER OF CHARGERS

If you do travel with multiple electronic devices, you will have to bear the additional burden of carrying all their chargers too. Check if a single charger can be used for multiple devices. You might also consider investing in a pocket charger. These small devices support multiple devices while keeping you charged on the go.

24. TRAVEL FRIENDLY APPS

Along with smart phones come numerous apps, which are immensely helpful in our travels. You name it and you have an app for it at hand – take pictures, sharing with friends and family, torch to light dark roads, maps, checking flight/train times, find hotels and many other things. Use these smart alternatives to traditional items like books to eliminate weight and save space.

I get ideas about what's essential
when packing my suitcase.

-Diane von Furstenberg

TRAVELLING WITH KIDS

25. BRING ALONG THE STROLLER

Kids might enjoy walking for a while but they soon tire out and a stroller is the just the right thing for them to rest in while you continue your tour. Strollers also double duty as a luggage carrier and shopping bag holder. Remember to pick a light weight, easy to handle brand of stroller. Better yet, find out in advance if you can rent a stroller at your destination.

26. BRING ONLY ENOUGH DIAPERS FOR YOUR TRIP

Diapers take up a lot of space and add to the weight of your luggage. Therefore it is advisable to carry just enough diapers to last through the trip and a few for afterwards, till you buy fresh stock at your destination. Unless of course you are travelling to a really remote area, in which case you have no choice but to carry the load. Otherwise diapers are something you will find pretty easily.

27. TAKE ONLY A COUPLE OF TOYS

Children are easily attracted by new things in their environment. While travelling they will find numerous 'new' objects to scrutinize and play with. Packing just one favorite toy is enough, or if there is no favorite toy leave out all of them in favor of stories or imaginary games.

28. CARRY KID FRIENDLY SNACKS

Create a small snack counter in your bag to store away quick bites for those sudden hunger pangs. Depending on the child's age this could include chocolates, raisins, dry fruits, granola bars or biscuits. Also keep a bottle of water handy for your little one.

These things do not add much weight and can be adjusted in a handbag or knapsack.

29. GAMES TO CARRY

Create some travel specific, imaginary games if you have slightly grown up children, like spot the attractions. Keep a coloring book and colors handy for in-flight or hotel time. Apps on your smart phone can keep the children engaged with cartoons and story books. Older children are often entertained by games available on phones or tablets. This cuts the weight of luggage down while keeping the kids entertained.

30. LET THE KIDS CARRY THEIR LOAD

A good thing is to start early sharing of responsibilities. Let your child pick a bag of his or her choice and pack it themselves. Keep tabs on what they are stuffing in their bags by asking if they will be using that item on the trip. It could start out being just an entertainment bag initially but with growing years they will learn to sort the useful from the superfluous. Children as little as four can maneuver a small trolley suitcase like a pro- their experience in pull along toys credit. If you are worried that you may be pulling it for them, you may want to start with a backpack.

31. DECIDE ON LOCATION FOR CHILDREN TO SLEEP

While on a trip you might not always get a crib at your destination, and carrying one will make life all the more difficult. Instead call ahead to see if there are any cribs or roll out beds for children. You may even put blankets on the floor. Weave them a story about camping and they will gladly sleep without any trouble.

32. GET BABY PRODUCTS DELIVERED AT YOUR DESTINATION

If you are absolutely paranoid about not getting your favourite variety of diaper or brand of baby food, check out online stores like amazon.com for services in your destination city. You can buy things online ahead of your travel and get them delivered to your hotel upon arrival.

33. FEEDING NEEDS OF YOUR INFANTS

If you are travelling with a breastfed infant, you save the trouble of carrying bottles and bottle sanitization kits. For special food, or medications, you may need to call ahead to make sure you have a refrigerator where you are staying.

34. FEEDING NEEDS OF YOUR TODDLER

With the progression from infancy to toddler, their dietary requirements too evolve. You will have to pack some snacks for travelling time. Fresh fruits and vegetables can be purchased at your destination. Most of the cities you travel to in whichever part of the world, will have baby food products and formulas, available at the local drug-store or the supermarket.

35. PICKING CLOTHES FOR YOUR BABY

Contrary to popular belief, babies can do without many changes of clothes. At the most pack 2 outfits per day. Pack mix and match type clothes for your little one as well. Pick things which are comfortable to wear and quick to dry.

36. SELECTING SHOES FOR YOUR BABY

Like outfits, kids can make do with two pairs of comfortable shoes. If you can get some water resistant shoes it will be best. To expedite drying wet shoes, you can stuff newspaper in them then wrap them with newspaper and leave them to dry overnight.

37. KEEP ONE CHANGE OF CLOTHES HANDY

Travelling with kids can be tricky. Keep a change of clothes for the kids and mum handy in your purse or tote bag. This takes a bit of space in your hand luggage but comes extremely handy in case there are any accidents or spills.

38. LEAVE BEHIND BABY ACCESSORIES

Baby accessories like their bed, bath tub, car seat, crib etc. should be left at home. Many hotels provide a crib on request, while car seats can be borrowed from friends or rented. Babies can be given a bath in the hotel sink or even in the adult bath tub with a little bit of water. If you bring a few bath toys, they can be used in the bath, pool, and out of water. They can also be sanitized easily in the sink.

39. CARRY A SMALL LOAD OF PLASTIC BAGS

With children around there are chances of a number of soiled clothes and diapers. These plastic bags help to sort the dirt from the clean inside your big bag.

These are very light weight and come in handy to other carry stuff as well at times.

PACK WITH A PURPOSE

40. PACKING FOR BUSINESS TRIPS

One neutral-colored suit should suffice. It can be paired with different shirts, ties and accessories for different occasions. One pair of black suit pants could be worn with a matching jacket for the office or with a snazzy top for dinner.

41. PACKING FOR A CRUISE

Most cruises have formal dinners, and that formal dress usually takes up a lot of space. However you might find a tuxedo to rent. For women, a short black dress with multiple accessory options will do the trick.

42. PACKING FOR A LONG TRIP OVER DIFFERENT CLIMATES

The secret packing mantra for travel over multiple climates is layering. Layering traps air around your body creating insulation against the cold. The same light t-shirt that is comfortable in a warmer climate can be the innermost layer in a colder climate.

REDUCE SOME MORE WEIGHT

43. LEAVE PRECIOUS THINGS AT HOME

Things that you would hate to lose or get damaged leave them at home. Precious jewelry, expensive gadgets or dresses, could be anything. You will not require these on your trip. Leave them at home and spare the load on your mind.

44. SEND SOUVENIRS BY MAIL

If you have spent all your money on purchasing souvenirs, carrying them back in the same bag that you brought along would be difficult. Either pack everything in another bag and check it in the airport or get everything shipped to your home. Use an international carrier for a secure transit, but this could be more expensive than the checking fees at the airport.

45. AVOID CARRYING BOOKS

Books equal to weight. There are many reading apps which you can download on your smart phone or tab.

Plus there are gadgets like Kindle and Nook that are thinner and lighter alternatives to your regular book.

CHECK, GET, SET, CHECK AGAIN

46. STRATEGIZE BEFORE PACKING

Create a travel list and prepare all that you think you need to carry along. Keep everything on your bed or floor before packing and then think through once again – do I really need that? Any item that meets this question can be avoided. Remove whatever you don't really need and pack the rest.

47. TEST YOUR LUGGAGE

Once you have fully packed for the trip take a test trip with your luggage. Take your bags and go to town for window shopping for an hour. If you enjoy your hour long trip it is good to go, if not, go home and reduce the load some more. Repeat this test till you hit the right weight.

48. ADD A ROLL OF DUCT TAPE

You might wonder why, when this book has been talking about reducing stuff, we're suddenly asking you to pack something totally unusual. This is because when you have limited supplies, duct tape is immensely helpful for small repairs – a broken bag, leaking zip-lock bag, broken sunglasses, you name it and duct tape can fix it, temporarily.

49. LIST OF ESSENTIAL ITEMS

Even though the emphasis is on packing light, there are things which have to be carried for any trip. Here is our list of essentials:

- Passport/Visa or any other ID

- Any other paper work that might be required on a trip like permits, hotel reservation confirmations etc.

- Medicines – all your prescription medicines and emergency kit, especially if you are travelling with children

- Medical or vaccination records

- Money in foreign currency if travelling to a different country

- Tickets- Email or Message them to your phone

50. MAKE THE MOST OF YOUR TRIP

Wherever you are going, whatever you hope to do we encourage you to embrace it whole-heartedly. Take in the scenery, the culture and above all, enjoy your time away from home.

On a long journey even a straw weighs heavy.

-Spanish Proverb

PACKING AND PLANNING TIPS

A Week before Leaving

- Arrange for someone to take care of pets and water plants

- Stop mail and newspaper

- Notify Credit Card companies where you are going.

- Change your thermostat settings

- Car inspected, oil is changed, and tires have the correct pressure.

- Passports and id is up to date.

- Pay bills.

- Copy important items and download travel Apps.

- Start collecting small bills for tips

Right Before Leaving

- Clean out refrigerator.

- Empty garbage cans.

- Lock windows.

- Make sure you have the right ID with you.

- Bring cash for tips.

- Remember travel documents.

- Lock door behind you.

- Remember wallet.

- Unplug items in house and pack chargers.

READ OTHER
GREATER THAN A TOURIST
BOOKS

Greater Than a Tourist San Miguel de Allende Guanajuato Mexico:
50 Travel Tips from a Local by Tom Peterson

Greater Than a Tourist – Lake George Area New York USA:
 50 Travel Tips from a Local by Janine Hirschklau

Greater Than a Tourist – Monterey California United States:
50 Travel Tips from a Local by Katie Begley

 Greater Than a Tourist – Chanai Crete Greece:
50 Travel Tips from a Local by Dimitra Papagrigoraki

Greater Than a Tourist – The Garden Route Western Cape Province
South Africa:
50 Travel Tips from a Local by Li-Anne McGregor van Aardt

Greater Than a Tourist – Sevilla Andalusia Spain:
50 Travel Tips from a Local by Gabi Gazon

Greater Than a Tourist – Kota Bharu Kelantan Malaysia:
50 Travel Tips from a Local by Aditi Shukla

Children's Book: Charlie the Cavalier Travels the World by Lisa
Rusczyk

> TOURIST

Visit Greater Than a Tourist for Free Travel Tips
http://GreaterThanATourist.com

Sign up for the Greater Than a Tourist Newsletter for discount days, new books, and travel information:
http://eepurl.com/cxspyf

Follow us on Facebook for tips, images, and ideas:
https://www.facebook.com/GreaterThanATourist

Follow us on Pinterest for travel tips and ideas:
http://pinterest.com/GreaterThanATourist

Follow us on Instagram for beautiful travel images:
http://Instagram.com/GreaterThanATourist

> TOURIST

Please leave your honest review of this book on Amazon and Goodreads. Please send your feedback to GreaterThanaTourist@gmail.com as we continue to improve the series. Thank you. We appreciate your positive and constructive feedback. Thank you.

METRIC CONVERSIONS

TEMPERATURE

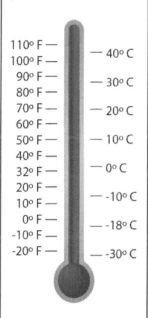

110° F —
100° F —   — 40° C
90° F —
80° F —   — 30° C
70° F —   — 20° C
60° F —
50° F —   — 10° C
40° F —
32° F —   — 0° C
20° F —
10° F —   — -10° C
0° F —
-10° F —   — -18° C
-20° F —   — -30° C

To convert F to C:

Subtract 32, and then multiply
by 5/9 or .5555.

To Convert C to F:

Multiply by 1.8
and then add 32.

32F = 0C

LIQUID VOLUME

To Convert:..................Multiply by
U.S. Gallons to Liters................ 3.8
U.S. Liters to Gallons 26
Imperial Gallons to U.S. Gallons 1.2
Imperial Gallons to Liters....... 4.55
Liters to Imperial Gallons 22
1 Liter = .26 U.S. Gallon
1 U.S. Gallon = 3.8 Liters

DISTANCE

To convert ....Multiply by
Inches to Centimeters 2.54
Centimeters to Inches 39
Feet to Meters...................... .3
Meters to Feet 3.28
Yards to Meters 91
Meters to Yards 1.09
Miles to Kilometers 1.61
Kilometers to Miles............ .62
1 Mile = 1.6 km
1 km = .62 Miles

WEIGHT

1 Ounce = .28 Grams
1 Pound = .4555 Kilograms
1 Gram = .04 Ounce
1 Kilogram = 2.2 Pounds

TRAVEL QUESTIONS

- Do you bring presents home to family or friends after a vacation?

- Do you get motion sick?

- Do you have a favorite billboard?

- Do you know what to do if there is a flat tire?

- Do you like a sun roof open?

- Do you like to eat in the car?

- Do you like to wear sun glasses in the car?

- Do you like toppings on your ice cream?

- Do you use public bathrooms?

- Did you bring your cell phone and does it have power?

- Do you have a form of identification with you?

- Have you ever been pulled over by a cop?

- Have you ever given money to a stranger on a road trip?

- Have you ever taken a road trip with animals?

- Have you ever went on a vacation alone?

- Have you ever run out of gas?

- If you could move to any place in the world, where would it be?

- If you could travel anywhere in the world, where would you travel?

- If you could travel in any vehicle, which one would it be?

- If you had three things to wish for from a magic genie, what would they be?

- If you have a driver's license, how many times did it take you to pass the test?

- What are you the most afraid of on vacation?

- What do you want to get away from the most when you are on vacation?

- What foods smells bad to you?

- What item to you bring on ever trip with you away from home?

- What makes you sleepy?

- What song would you love to hear on the radio when you're cruising on the highway?

- What travel job would you want the least?

- What will you miss most while you are away from home?

- What is something you always wanted to try?

- What is the best road side attraction that you ever saw?

- What is the farthest distance you ever biked?

- What is the farthest distance you ever walked?

- What is the weirdest thing you needed to buy while on vacation?

- What is your favorite candy?

- What is your favorite color car?

- What is your favorite family vacation?

- What is your favorite food in the world?

- What is your favorite gas station drink or food?

- What is your favorite license plate design?

- What is your favorite restaurant in the world?

- What is your favorite smell?

- What is your favorite song?

- What is your favorite sound that nature makes?

- What is your favorite thing to bring home from a vacation?

- What is your favorite vacation with friends?

- What is your favorite way to relax?

- What is your favorite weather conditions while driving?

- Where in the world would you rather never get to travel?

- Where is the farthest place you ever traveled in a car?

- Where is the farthest place you ever went North, South, East and West?

- Where is your favorite place in the world?

- Who is your favorite singer?

- Who taught you how to drive?

- Who will you miss the most while you are away?

- Who if the first person you will call when you get to your destination?

- Who brought you on your first vacation?

- Who likes to travel the most in your life?

- Would you rather be hot or cold?

- Would you rather drive above, below, or at the speed limited?

- Would you rather drive on a highway or a back road?

- Would you rather go on a train or a boat?

- Would you rather go to the beach or the woods?

TRAVEL BUCKET LIST

1.

2.

3.

4.

5.

6.

7.

8.

9.

10.

NOTES

Printed in Great Britain
by Amazon